John Aston Whitlock

A Brief and Popular History of the Hospital of God's House,

Southampton

John Aston Whitlock

A Brief and Popular History of the Hospital of God's House, Southampton

ISBN/EAN: 9783337161347

Printed in Europe, USA, Canada, Australia, Japan

Cover: Foto ©Andreas Hilbeck / pixelio.de

More available books at **www.hansebooks.com**

A

Brief and Popular History

OF THE

HOSPITAL OF GOD'S HOUSE

SOUTHAMPTON.

BY

THE REV. J. ASTON WHITLOCK, M.A.,

Vicar of Holy Rood & Chaplain of God's House, Southampton.

SOUTHAMPTON :

HENRY MARCH GILBERT, YE OLDE BOKE SHOPPE,

26, ABOVE BAR.

PREFACE.

IN order not to weary the eye of the reader I have troubled him with as few footnotes, and inverted commas as possible ; and the very small amount of Mediæval Latin, which is embodied in the text, has been always translated. My chief authorities, which I have myself examined, or my friends for me, are as follows (some of them have not always rewarded our labours) : Great Roll of the Pipe ; Madox, History of the Exchequer ; Rotuli Chartarum in Turri Londinensi, ed. T. Duffus Hardy; Eyton's Itinerary of Henry II. ; Woodward's History of Hampshire ; Davies' History of Southampton ; Hants Historical Records ; the Cecil Papers at Hatfield; Dugdale's Monasticon, &c.

My obligations and thanks are due to the following gentlemen for kindly help and suggestions: the Librarians at the British Museum, the Librarian at Hatfield House, the Librarian at Lambeth Palace, the Librarian at the Hartley Institute, the Very Rev. the Dean of Winchester, the Provost of Queen's Coll., Oxford, Rev. J. Silvester Davies, T. W. Shore, Esq., F.G.S., the Town Clerk of Southampton, and others.

" *Adsta, atque Athenas antiquum opulentum oppidum*
Contempla ; age, Templum Cereris ad lævam adspice.
ENNIUS.

Pause here, and scan the rich and antique Hamptone,
And mark the God's House Hostel on the left.
FREE TRANSLATION.

" The Beauty of Usefulness."

PREFACE TO THE LATE PRINCE CONSORT'S
SPEECHES.

INTRODUCTORY.

B EFORE entering upon the history of Domus
Dei—Maison Dieu—or God's House, Southampton, the following prefatory remarks will, I
think, prove not uninteresting to the reader.

The English people from very early times were
great travellers and went much abroad. The
Crusades, especially that one in which Richard
Cœur de Lion was engaged, have much to answer
for in fostering this vagrom spirit. It may be quite
true that—

> " Men are made to roam—
> Madam, it hath been always thus ;
> They are athirst for mountains and sea-foam :
> Heirs of the world, what wonder if perchance
> They long to see their grand inheritance."

Still, there can be no doubt that those marauding
expeditions, combined with the religious element,
added momentum to this natural tendency, and
helped to turn feeling and desire into actuality.
The soldiers and their comrades had rare stories to
tell on their return ; and the account of the many
"mervaylles" and "fayre miracles," which they
came across in the continental towns and in the
Holy Land, whetted the appetite for foreign travel.
The Spirit of Religion, too, fostered by Holy
Church, imparted additional zest—the merit of
works, chiefly of slaying a " Sarazin " or of seeing

Jerusalem and other sacred places with all their hallowed associations,—has much to answer for in contributing to sharpen and satisfy their inborn craving for roaming about. To have gazed upon and perhaps even to have reverentially kissed the body of St. James the Great at Compostella, the ear of St. Peter at Venice, the very manger itself at Bethlehem, one of the nails of the Cross, or—highest fulfilment of all ardent hopes—a chip of the cross itself,—this was indeed the satisfaction of a soul-consuming craving, enough for a life-time, and—better still—helped the "Christian" way-farer many steps towards heaven. The moon was assigned as their Planet, because of the "mone's disposicion" to wander and change : for as Caxton saith—"We Englysshe men have been borne under the domynacion of the mone, whiche is never sted-faste but ever waverynge."

A pilgrimage of this kind was not to be lightly undertaken. Manuals of the French language, hitherto restricted to the higher classes, "who knew the Romance better than Latin," were com-posed and prepared for the Pilgrims. French would carry them through the Continent, and the Franks in Palestine spoke that language. Mediæval writers declare deploringly that the English were forgetting their own tongue : for they were em-ploying competent persons to compile handbooks, whereby they might be able "to speak the sweet French, which is the finest and most graceful lan-guage, the noblest to speak, of any in the world after Latin of the Schools, and is better prized and loved than any other by all men ; for God made it sweet and loveable chiefly to His own Praise and Honour. And therefore it may well compare with

the language of the Angels in Heaven, on account
of its great sweetness and beauty."

Thus equipped, we will suppose a monk—or
some such other holy man—to start forth on pilgrimage from his monastery. His whole travelling
gear appears to have consisted of "a scrippe and
a burdon." The former was a bag to contain
"vittelles"—no doubt hardy fare—or anything
else of a sacred and more valuable nature. The
latter was the Pilgrim's Staff, shaped like the
modern alpenstock. Starting from his monastery,
he is escorted by divers "Bretheren and Sisteren"
as far as the city gates—or, if the town be on the
sea-coast, to the place of embarcation. There they
take a tender and tearful farewell, not altogether
unmixed with a little pious envy, and so commend
him to the "Proteccion of Godde and the Grace of
oure Ladye."

Our pilgrim will presently find that he is not
likely to be alone and solitary ; on shipboard he is
merely one of other such wayfarers, and he has
many companions in "traveyle." On arriving (say)
at Calais he makes his way to the Maison Dieu,
where he is "entreated courteously" and hospitably,
and furthered on his journey. Thus we see the
object of the erection of those hostels, and infer
rightly that they are to be found chiefly at seaport
towns, such as Dover, Southampton, Calais, Venice,
&c. After Calais, the pilgrims scattered in various
directions, either according to a preconcerted plan,
or as their own will might at the time direct. But
of course they always sought towns on the route to
the Holy Land (if they were going thither), or those
celebrated for "mervaylles," miracles, and strange
sights, such as acted as bracing tonics to their

pious enthusiasm. At Amiens there was the head of John the Baptist to be reverently gazed upon: but Sir John de Mandeville was dreadfully scandalized, and his childlike faith received a rude shock at Constantinople, where *another* head of the Baptist, equally genuine, was presented to him for the usual homage! Compostella, as I have already said, could shew the body of St. James. Another town boasted of a feather from the wing of the Angel Gabriel, and also a ray from the light of the Magi's star in the East, caught and secured in a phial, closely corked up and sealed! Generally, our Pilgrim would trudge on to Venice, where he would rest awhile in the Maison Dieu, and make preparation for crossing the sea to Cyprus and Palestine. Venice was by no means behind in its "fayre mervaylles." In this "most excellent, noble, great, and fine town, all seated in the sea, are the arm of our Lord St. George; one of the water-pots of Cana; one ear of St. Paul; three of the stones thrown at St. Stephen; and the body of St. Mark, which is a very fine and noble thing." But its Maison Dieu was not to be outdone even by such "merveylles," for it possessed a "merveylle" of its own, "surpassing fayre"—nothing less than "one of the molar teeth of a Giant that was called Goliath, which Giant David killed; and, know you, that this tooth is more than half a foot long, and weigheth twelve pounds!!"

When the Pilgrim has thus far satisfied his hungry soul, he next addresses his energies to the stormy passage across the Adriatic and Mediterranean Seas to Famagusta and Jaffa. As the entertainment on board ship is of a somewhat rude nature, savouring of discomfort, he is recommended "to by at Venyse a fedyr bedde, a matres, too pylwys, too peyre schetis, and a qwylt, and ye schal pay iii dokettis " (ducats). If he should, on his return, bring them back in fair condition he will receive for them " one doket and halfe ayen " (again). As the food on board was generally of the coarsest description, and such as ordinary teeth could hardly masticate and tender stomachs digest ; especially too, as he will be sure to suffer from mal-de-mer, he is advised " to by a cage for half-a-dozen hennys or chekyn to ete of youre owne "— also some pepper, saffron, and spices for " comfortatyngs " and " consolacion " generally. And especially " beware of dyurse frutys " in the Holy Land ; " for they gender a blody fluxe ; and yf an Englyschman have that sykenes, hyt is a merveylle and scape hyt but he dye thereof."

Let us now suppose that our Pilgrim has accomplished the object of his Pilgrimage, and prepares once again to turn his face homewards. With what joy, not unmixed with awe, will he be welcomed back to his monastery! Arriving at Dover or Southampton he will land in company with fellow-pilgrims, possibly with some of Cœur de Lion's soldiers, certainly with foreign chapmen and " riche marchantz." He makes his way to the Maison Dieu, where water is provided for the washing of his begrimed and tired feet, and " refection" is set before him. In due course he attends the Chapel service, and offers thanks for the protecting care of " Godde, owre Ladye, and St. Julian," the Patron Saint of Travellers and Pilgrims. After a short rest, the holy man starts for his monastery. The news of his return thither anticipates him, and on his arrival at the City

Gates he is again met and escorted with due
honour to his old home by the " Bretheren and
Sisteren." Here for the weary man is a repetition
of the feet-washing, the refection, and the Giving
of Thanks. And then he begins to pour forth some
of the treasures of his Pilgrim experiences. Besides
those " fayre merveylles " at Amiens, Venice and
other cities, his eyes have looked in Palestine upon
the rudder of St. Peter's boat on the Lake of
Gennesaret ; the little school on the hill where our
Ladye, as a young girl, received her education ;
the place where the water had been warmed,
wherewith the Blessed Lord had washed His dis-
ciples' feet ; the Pool into which the wicked Herod
had thrown the Innocents ;—to say nothing of
Bethlehem with its Manger—the Holy Sepulchre—
the Hill of Shame—and the Mount of Olives.
Then, too, he will descant on the perils and dangers
to which he was exposed by sea and by land from
storms and leaky ships ; from robbers, and
murderous, treacherous " Sarsanes ; " from dragons
and from divers demons—all for the salvation of
his soul and the love of " Jesu Crist."

What a strange, wonderful story it all was !
How it would wile away many a long winter's
evening ! No doubt it lost nothing of the mar-
vellous in its recital ! Nevertheless, how full of
edification to the childlike audience, of consolation
to the narrator's soul, of benefit and glory to Holy
Church.

The rage for Pilgrimages reached its culminating
point in the reign of Richard II. About this era
flourished Geoffrey Chaucer, who, in his " Canterbury Tales," gives us an amusing insight into the
character and conduct of the Pilgrims. But Kings

and Counsellors were inclined to look upon these religious wayfarers with some disfavour. They considered that this going on Pilgrimage drew the inhabitants of the villages to towns where there were shrines, and added to an already crowded population; while the villages were thus denuded of their inhabitants, the roads became infested with idlers, cut-throats, and "sturdy beggars." Imposters and pious hypocrites everywhere abounded. Agriculture was neglected, and work and honest labour made way for idleness, beggary, and poverty, dependent on the almsgiving of the Faithful. It was even said that more Englishmen could be found abroad on the Continent than in England itself. This, of course, deprived the King of the services of his own subjects, and harm and loss thereby accrued to the kingdom. At length, in the reign of Richard II. (1377-1399), matters came to such a climax, that no one was permitted to go on Pilgrimage without a Government "pass ; " and these "passes" were available only at certain Ports, of which Southampton was one. Pilgrimages virtually received their death-blow at the Reformation. They have, of course, been revived frome time to time in more modern days, but under circumstances and conditions so different from those of our ancient forefathers, that no further allusion need be made to them. This portion of our subject may therefore be drawn to a close. Enough has been said to show the object which " Pious Founders " had in view, when they established and endowed a Maison Dieu in seaport towns.

[*The reader's attention is directed to "Jusserand's Wayfaring Life in XIVth Century."*]

Hospital of God's House.

CHAPTER I.

AFTER the preliminary chapter on Pilgrimages we can now turn our attention with all the greater interest to our Hospital of God's House. But it will be necessary, after dealing with the somewhat dry details of its foundation, to touch briefly on the trade and commerce of the town of Southampton, inasmuch as this forms a connecting link between the Hospital and the Huguenots. For, as we shall see in due course, the Hospital Chapel of St. Julian was assigned, during the reign of Queen Elizabeth, to those persecuted exiles, in order that they might enjoy freedom to worship God according to their own "use" and rites and ceremonies. Within its sacred walls many of the Huguenot ministers lie interred.

We will first transcribe the account given by the antiquary, John Leland, Chaplain and Librarian to King Henry VIII.

"There is a Hospitale yn the Town toward the South, caullyd Goddeshouse, whereyn is a Chapelle, dedicate to Saynte Juliane, the Bishop.

The Hospitale was founded by 2 Marchaunts, beyng Bretherne . . . . the one was caullyd Ge . . . the other Protasius of . . . . day by like lihood that they were borne. These 2 3 Brethren, as I then lerned, dwellyd in the very Place wher the Hospitale is now, at such tyme as old Hampton was brent by Pyrates. These 2 Brethern for Goddes sake caused their house to be turned to an Hospitale for poore Folkes, and endowed it with sum landes."

So far old Leland. The reader will observe
that there are gaps in his manuscript, that he was
apparently in some doubt as to the number of the
brothers, and that he has managed to confuse the
two, through similarity of name, with the two mar-
tyrs of Rome, Gervasius and Protasius, whose remains were believed to have been discovered by St.
Ambrose, by whom they were buried in his newly-
founded Cathedral at Milan, of which they became
the patron saints. At any rate no Protasius is
discoverable in connection with God's House. So
we will leave our inexact historian and endeavour
to get at the true account from existing ancient
manuscripts and records.

The Hospice, or Hospital of God's House—
Domus Dei or Maison Dieu—was founded at the
close of the 12th Century, about the year 1185, by
one, Gervase or Gervaise, Burgess and Portreeve
of Southampton. His office was dignified and
honourable ; his duties were onerous and full of
responsibility; and from his subsequent surname
(le Riche) we may infer that he was a man of sub-
stance. In the Norman or Mediæval Latin of that
period, he is named " Præpositus de Sudhanton."
This office of " Portreeve " appears to correspond
with that of our modern " Mayor," and its duties
consisted chiefly in clearing foreign ships in the
matter of harbour-dues, and forwarding an account
of them to the king. In some of the records of that
period his name repeatedly occurs, e.g., " Et
Gervâs de tūro," in full, "Gervasius de Thesauro,"
that is—Gervase who presides over the Treasure.
Hence our term " Treasurer." There is a note to
the effect that " Nigellus of Havana* (i.e., Copenhagen) owes L. marks for the interchange of Mer-
chandise which he has had with Gervasius of
Hanton." And again—" In the clearing of the

* This is probably a mistake for Havnia, the Latin name of
Copenhagen.

INTERIOR OF CHAPEL.

FROM A PHOTO BY DEBENHAM & SMITH.

p. 16.

King's yacht, when the Duke of Saxony and the Queen crossed the Channel, it cost viii.*l* and x.*s* by writ of Ranulf of Glanville," (that is, apparently, the payment was made on Ranulf's letter, cheque or bill) and " Gervase, Portreeve of Sudhampton, gives the receipt." It would only tire the reader to repeat these small notices, which are interesting, however, so far as they contribute to our knowledge of the man and his duties. Most of them are dated in Henry II.'s reign ; but though Henry frequently landed at or departed from Southampton on his visits to and from his Continental kingdoms, there does not seem to be any mention of Gervasius in " Henry II.'s Itinerary." His name, however, occurs during Richard I.'s reign in connection with other matters besides sending in accounts. Richard was rebuilding and enlarging Portsmouth, and made a grant of a " placea "—an unoccupied piece of land—to anyone, free of charge, who would build a tenement thereon. Such a spot he conferred upon our Gervase, who went no further, however, than shooting a heap of stones on his piece of land, no doubt intending at a future time to make further use of the materials. But he seems to have died soon after, for his " widow " is referred to (as we shall see presently) about the year 1204. Some interest is nevertheless attached to this " placea," which was near the quay,—" super kaiam "—inasmuch as, at the death of Gervase, the Sheriff of Hants got it from the king, and, having bestowed it on the Prior of Portsmouth, an action was brought in the year 1212, to see whether the Sheriff had unjustly dis-seized the Master of the Hospital in Southampton of the free tenement which he held at Portsmouth.

The exact date of this good man's death cannot be stated, but in the year 1204 a messuage, which had been purchased from Isabella, the widow (quondam uxorem Gervasii) of Gervase, and his heir, was confirmed to the buyer, Geoffrey, son of Peter, Earl of Essex, by King John. Although a son Roger is mentioned, he must have died in early life, as we unexpectedly read of an heir in this very document, called Walter,* son of Berengarius (scilicet Walter, fil. Berengarii). The witnesses to this Royal Script are, " R., Earl of Chester (comes Castrensis), Hugo de Nevill, Robert de Veteriponte, Peter de Stok and John de Stok." It was issued " xxi. die Aprilis anno regni nostri quinto," —on the 21st day of April in the 5th year of our reign. (King John ascended the throne in the year 1199.) This " Charta " of King John is worthy of quotation for two reasons : while it adds somewhat to our knowledge of Gervase's family, it also suggests a reason for so influential a citizen never having been elected to the chief magistracy. We have seen that he died somewhere about the year 1203 or 4. Whereas Southampton was not incorporated until the year 1205, when there are good reasons for surmising that a citizen, probably prominent at the time, though utterly unknown to *us*, named Acon or Azon, was elected first mayor. It is recorded that Gervase had an only brother, Roger (possibly a twin, possibly Leland's Protasius), who was the first Warden of God's House. But beyond this passing, almost legendary, notice, nothing more is recorded or known of him. *(Appendix I.)*

It may interest the reader to find that the name of Gervase is not an uncommon one in early history. There was an Abbess of Romsey, in the 14th Century, by name Joan Gervase. Another Gervase was a lay-brother of Romsey. Gervasius appears more than once in the Rolls of Hyde

---

* Two nephews, or perhaps grandsons, are mentioned in the old records, Walter and Thomas If they were grandsons, Roger would most likely be a younger son of Gervase. In the reign of Edward II., a Sir Yngebrand Berengir is mentioned in the God's House Archives.

Abbey. A William Gerveys was one of the Jurats
of the Parish of Baddesley. The name re-appears
(I may be pardoned for adding this), in these modern days in Sir George Gervis Tapps Meyrick, Bart.;
as Le Riche does in the family of Rich—both resident in the County of Hants—and both contributors
to the prosperity and glory of their native land.
It is just possible that the name of Gervase also
lies embedded and veiled in that of Jervois—which
presents itself in manifold and diverse forms. *

* Additional notes on the family of Gervase will be found
in the Appendix.

CHAPTER II.

A very natural question here arises : What impulse
moved the good Gervase to found his hospital ?
Was he urged thereto by a vision, or the suggestion
of a pious wife ? Was he prompted by the death
of a son or daughter, leaving him mourning and
desolate ? Was the foundation a thank-offering
for recovery from a dangerous illness, or for some
great mercies received ? These are questions which
cannot now be answered. In those days private
diaries were rare and have not survived ; and pub-
lic records do not abound in such superfluous
explanations. The probability is, that from the
experience of his official duties, his tender heart
was touched by the almost daily sight of so much
poverty, sickness, and misery disembarking at the
Port, and that such a good work as the founding
of the Hospice, would advance the salvation of his
soul, and tend to the glory of " Godde " and the
honour of " owre Ladye."

The tradition, to which Leland refers, of the
Hospital occupying the site of the founder's private
residence, is not an unreasonable one. As Portreeve, he would be likely to live near the scene of
his duties. In his day the house lay perfectly open,
confronting the harbour. There was then no ob-
structive wall running along Winkle Street from
(roughly speaking) the Water Gate to God's House
Gateway. The Portreeve would step out of his
house, through the wicket-gate, at once upon a
pier or quay, against which, at high tide, the
waters lapped, and where the official vessel *(navis
Præpositi)* awaited him for embarcation. Behind,
and at the side of his house, along the present High
Street, and up to Gloucester Square, stretched the

RESIDENCE OF THE SISTERS.

FROM A PHOTO BY DEBENHAM & SMITH.

P. 30.

garden and orchards. And close by, at the other side, lay the Bowling Green, where we can imagine him chasing away his weariness and anxieties—a healthy pastime, that of bowls, in which brave men indulged in more modern times, before they went on board ship to fight and win battles.

The present buildings, we may suppose, are the successors of similar structures reared at the foundation of the Hospital. They form a small quadrangle with grass-plot and trees in the centre. On the north side lie the residences of the "sisters"—four under one roof. Exactly opposite, on the south side, is the chapel. The Warden's House, on the west, faces the "brothers'" residences on the east—the latter being an exact counterpart of those of the "sisters." Within such circumscribed limits does the present "Hospital" lie ; but in its former condition it must have stretched out behind the Warden's House, along the High Street, and up to Gloucester Square, where in ancient times was a Friary of Franciscan Minorites, from which the God's House domain was separated by a mound of earth. Here, no doubt, stood the refectory, the kitchen, and the infirmary—buildings which have long ago vanished. There must, too, have been a grave-yard or cemetery, though no traces of it can now be found. The charges for a funeral are given below, and one can only conjecture that it took place within the precincts of our "Hospital." No place of sepulture, however, is mentioned. That there were other buildings, besides those which now exist, in connection with the "Hospital," may be regarded as a certainty. In the first place they are mentioned in the old records. But besides this, there is an old Norman doorway, on the left hand as you enter the archway, exactly opposite the west door of the Chapel. It is now blocked up and covered with cement ; but it must evidently have been the entrance to some large building, whose site is now occupied by coal-cellars. If (again) the reader will, with the permission of the occupier of No. 80, High Street, penetrate to the furthest corner of the back yard, turn round, and literally lift up his eyes, he will see one of the very few Norman chimneys which now survive in our land. (Two others still exist—at Lincoln and at Christchurch, Hants; a fourth, at Warnford Manor House, in this county, has lately fallen). If my reader will now re-enter the back room of the house, he will see that this enormous chimney communicates with what has been turned into a closet or cupboard, but which was undoubtedly at some early period, a capacious fireplace. It could only have been needed for a vast establishment; and we cannot be far from the truth, in believing that it belonged to the kitchen of our "Hospital;" and we may assume, with fair probability of certainty, that the Refectory was not far off.

The *Warden's House* is somewhat capacious, long but without depth; and to it a garden is attached. It has been divided into two dwellings which are let to tenants wholly unconnected with the "Hospital." A solid iron railing now separates it from the Quadrangle, into which there is no entrance from that side.

The *Residences of the "Bretheren and Sisteren"* consist, each, of one sitting-room, one bed-room, and a small kitchen or scullery, and afford ample room and a comfortable home for one person. The two "several" blocks of buildings, on the north and east side, are assigned, the former to the "Sisters," the latter to the "Brothers." The one block is an exact counterpart to the other; therefore the same description will apply to both. Two sets of rooms are on the ground floor; and by an intermediate staircase you ascend to the two sets over them. These residences the four "Sisters" and four "Brothers"—whose numbers are specified by charter of Queen Elizabeth—occupy, free of rent, rates, taxes, and repairs; and the whole institution is supervised by a chaplain, appointed by Queen's College—usually one of the clergy of the town. He does not, however, reside at God's House.

While we are dealing with this part of the subject, the allowance made to the inmates by Queen's College may be here stated.

To each weekly   ....   11s.

Divided amongst all :

Per Annum, Shaving Money ....   10s.
   ,,   ,, Meade Money   ....   12s.
Quarterly, Soap Money   ....   6s. 8d.

Besides this, old townsmen of " pious memory " have left the following grants for their benefit :

Sadleirs' Charity, at Christmas   £2 13s. 4d.
Fifield's   ,,   to be expended
                       in coals £6 16s. 0d.
Gibbon's   ,,   paid in coin.... £20 16s. 0d.

The " Bretheren and Sisteren " are, therefore, not ill-cared for, and the Institution in many respects offers comforts and freedom from anxiety, without any loss of self-respect, to those who have reached the " sere and yellow leaf " time of life. Nor is the Hospital to be regarded as a mere appendage to the workhouse. Great care is exercised by the College in their appointment to vacancies, and the successful candidates are usually selected from a respectable class of society, for whom the workhouse was never intended, who have fallen into straitened circumstances, and yet naturally shrink from becoming a burden to their friends or relations in the matter of maintenance : decayed tradesmen, aged schoolmistresses, employés at the Ordnance Office, broken in health, yet ineligible to a pension from Government ; these and such others have found a comfortable home for their remaining days within these hospitable walls.

It ought to be explained that the " *shaving money* " which the *ladies* (!) receive as well as the beard-growing members of the community, an item which may puzzle most of my readers, is no doubt a relic of the payment to the *Barber-Surgeon*, who in past times was a very important personage indeed, and usually attached to large institutions and establishments.

I have been informed that at Jesus College, Oxford, the head porter always resided at the lodge, and, until quite a recent period, was the barber of the College.

We may now turn our attention to the Chapel.

The *Chapel*, dedicated to St. Julian, the Patron Saint of Travellers and Wayfarers, of whom the reader will find a short account at the end of this chapter, was rebuilt with the pensioners' residences in 1861. It was restored on the foundations of the old chapel ; but a quatrefoil insertion, breast-high, in the S.W. corner of the sacred building, outside the gate-tower, and through which a view of the interior could be obtained without entering it, has not been repeated in the restored portion. Probably it was intended for lepers or other outcasts, who could thus see the High Altar and could be present, at least, in spirit during the hours of worship. Except as a matter of archæology, it had served its purpose, and its removal would no longer offer a temptation to inquisitive idlers. The Chapel is some 60 feet long by about 20 feet broad, lighted by plain Norman windows, having a chancel arch of the early English period, as it was verging on to the decorative style of architecture. The handsome Reredos and Holy Table were placed there, with permission of the College, by members of the French Protestant congregation, to whom most of the furniture belongs. With one exception, all the tablets are in memory of French pasteurs, who from the days of the Huguenots have ministered there—of whom more hereafter.

A beautiful brass fastened to a mahogany slab, about three feet long, with a curious head of alabaster attached, is stated to be the figure of Wallerand Thevelin, one of the French ministers in 1584. But the dress points to a much earlier period, and it no doubt represents one of the priests or chaplains of the 13th or 14th century.

There is a small head, carved in stone, over the (inside of) west door, of which I can learn nothing. If it be in its original position, it may have served as a stand for a lamp, or a small statue of St. Julian, or of " owre Ladye."

The west door was re-opened about 20 years ago, for the better accommodation of the worshippers. Until then there had been only one entrance to the Chapel, viz., on the north side, from the "Quad." Curiously, there is a notice in one of the ancient rolls, in the year 1299, to this effect :—
" A new door for the new Chapel towards the west." And again, in the record of the God's House expenses — " A carpenter for door west of new chapel, 4d. ; with vittels at the warden's expense."

Outside, in the south-east corner of the Quadrangle, there are remains of an old chapel ; but no one can give me any information about them, except that they were portions taken from St. Julian's at its restoration in 1861, and placed there for neatness. But this is merely conjecture. The pillar in the adjacent wall has evidently been there for a long period.

I must now ask the reader to revert once again to the *Tablets*, that he may learn something about *the* one of exceptional interest. It records the following incident,—

" Richard, Earl of Cambridge, Lord Scrope of Masham, and

Sir Tho. Gray of Northumberland, conspired to murder King
Henry V. in this Town, as he was preparing to sail with his army
against Charles VI. of France, for which conspiracy they were
executed, and buried near this place in the year MCCCCXV."

A few lines, copied from " Local Notes and
Queries," will briefly explain this conspiracy. It
appears that after these three gentlemen were found
out and taken, they very naturally made confession
in hopes of obtaining the King's pardon. The plot
was this. They were to carry Edmund, Earl of
March, into Wales, and get him to assume the
sovereignty, if it was found to be true (as some
professed to doubt) that Richard II. was really
dead. The conspirators were to take with them a
banner of the arms of England, and a certain crown
of Spain, set upon a palet, which had been placed
in pawn by the King, to the Earl of Cambridge.
Other confederates at the same time were to bring
Thomas de Trumpington (the pretended Richard
II.) from Scotland, along with Henry Percy (son of
Hotspur), while the king's castles were seized in
Wales, and proclamations issued against him as
an usurper. The plot began just before the as-
sembling of the soldiers at Southampton. Sir
Thomas Gray states how he came on his journey
to his lodging at Hambledon, and thence on to
Hampton. The Earl of March was staying at
Hamul in the Hoke (apparently Hamble), and
there these two men with the Earl of Cambridge
discussed the subject of the conspiracy. Afterwards, Lord Scrope, who had not been then
present, met them at the "fere of Hickys"
(perhaps Itchen Ferry), and there they discussed
the situation. Subsequently, adds Sir Thomas
Gray, " on the morow ye Erle of Cambridge
and I in ye Devels name roden to ye Hamull
of ye Hoke, and yer spake with ye Erle of March."
It turned out, however, that Henry and his emis-
saries were on their track, and his Satanic Majesty

did not give much help to the conspirators. They were soon captured; and Henry, who did not usually let the grass grow under his feet, being a man of despatch, as soon as he had wormed out of them by confession all that he wanted, had the three chief plotters executed, somewhere above the Bar Gate. The fact was, that the Earl of March had himself divulged the plot to the King.

As a confirmation of the story and the inscription, a gigantic skeleton was found, lying full length, under the chancel floor of St. Julian's. His head was not in the place where the human head usually grows, but had been carefully placed between his knees. Evidently, these were the remains of one of the conspirators—which, we cannot with certainty affirm—but probably of the Earl of Cambridge. He was grandfather of King Edward IV., of whom more anon.

Additional Note on St. Julian.

According to Ecclesiastical tradition there were at least twelve Saints of this name. Ours, however, was the son of wealthy parents, living in Southern France. He was, like most young men of the day, a great huntsman, and devoted to the pleasures of the chase. As he was on one occasion pursuing a doe, the poor exhausted creature, suddenly turning towards him, became vocal and prophesied that he would be the murderer of his parents. This prophecy he unwittingly and unexpectedly fulfilled, at which he was so horrified that he left home with his young wife, resolving to do penance and expiate his crime by the good deeds of a hermit's life. They wandered far away from home, until they reached the banks of a rapidly-flowing river. Here he built a hut, and set up a ferry-boat, and added another hut as an Infirmary or Hospital for the sick and afflicted, upon whom he and his wife attended, as well as ferried the wayfarers, free of charge. One day a leper came to be ferried over, and our ferryman not only willingly received him into his boat, but took him up in his arms, and carried him to the hospital. Presently, a miraculous light, a halo, seemed to betoken a Divine Person in the leper ; and so we are not surprised to find that the good man and his wife heard a voice, soon after, declaring that he had made sufficient expiation and that his great sin was wholly forgiven. I am not sure that he ever was made a bishop, as Leland says ; but there is no doubt that they both died in the odour of sanctity.

Such is the traditionary life of St. Julian, Hospitator, patron saint of wayfarers, of ferrymen and boatmen, and of travelling minstrels, who wandered about from door to door. In sacred Art he is represented in rich secular attire, as a cavalier or courtier, young, with a mild and melancholy expression ; often holds a hunting horn in his hand, and a stag behind him or at his feet. Sometimes he is delineated in the garb of a hermit, accompanied by the stag, with generally a river and boat in the background. There are pictures of him ferrying travellers over a stream, while his wife stands at the door, holding a light :—for he worked by night as well as by day.

The finest picture of him is still to be seen at the Pitti Palace, Florence ; and his story is also told in a series of subjects on one of the windows of Rouen Cathedral, presented by the Company or Guild of Boatmen (Bateliers-pecheurs) of that city, in the XIVth Century.—*Chiefly from Mrs. Jameson's History of Sacred and Legendary Art.*

CHAPTER III.

GERVASE, having founded his " Hospital," seems to have arranged its internal economy somewhat upon the lines of Rahere's great Hospital of St. Bartholomew, in London. (Rahere had been Henry the First's Jester and Chief Minstrel).

The resident members of the " Hospital " consisted of a custos or warden, two or more priests, three or more brethren, some ten sisters, three or more poor men and women—who were to make themselves generally useful according to their health and strength. Besides these, there were various officials and servants necessary for so large an establishment : as, for instance, cook, barber-surgeon, laundress, dairymaid, cowherd, shepherd, brewer, swineherd, and so forth. There appears to have been a large body of men, partially non-resident, who, acting as under-stewards, managed the various properties of the " Hospital," and had to give account thereof to the warden. Attached to the establishment also were others, non-resident, living on the various farms and manors, and being unpaid, subsisted on the produce of the land which they tilled.

For the maintenance of the " Hospital " the founder bestowed on it grants of land, farms, manors, messuages, &c., which were supplemented in after years by further bequests made by royal and other " pious " donors. Some of these lands lay round about and in the neighbourhood of God's House, and are now covered with houses. Other landed property was situated further afield—at Stoneham, West End, Botley, also in Portsmouth, Dorset, and the Isle of Wight.

The "Sisters" and other females were expected
to make themselves useful in the "Hospital" by
nursing the sick, and offering frequent prayers.
They received a farthing per day for clothing, and
an extra payment for exceptional acts and duties,
such as abstaining from meat for a certain period.
The "Brethren," too, were not allowed to be idle;
but, when not required at home, were sent to look
after the interests of the establishment at its various tenements and farms, as occasion might
require.

The pauper portion of the community received,
besides their food, one farthing every two days.
They were, however, allowed to make additions to
this munificent sum by engaging in extra employ-
ment. Thus : one became a gate-keeper, another
helped at harvest time to reap corn, a third
assisted at some menial work, and at the end of
the year was presented with two pairs of shoes of
the value of xijd.

The "Brethren and Sisters" were also to receive the travellers, wayfarers, and pilgrims, on
their embarkation and debarkation, or on their
journey generally, to wait upon them in the refectory, and to tend them, if sick, in the infirmary.
Lepers, however, appear to have been excluded
from the latter building, as there was a special
leper hospital already in existence, founded by the
burgesses, and dedicated to St. Mary Magdalene,
in the upper part of the town, situated in that
space of ground which now goes by the name of
the Mar(y)lands. Special directions were laid
down for religious "acts" and "uses," amongst
others the recitation of the "Angelorum Salutatio,"
and the "Pater noster" by the "Brethren and
Sisters" 180 times a day.

The religious rule was that of St. Augustine.
The first warden is said to have been the Founder's
brother, Roger. He bestowed the patronage (what-

ever that included) upon the Bishop of Winchester. Patronage has always had its perils. Even a late Lord Chancellor is reported to have said that he never knew the blessings of patronage until he was cursed with it. A certain Bishop of Winchester in the 13th century may have thought and said the same. For in the year 1290, the sheriff, on the death of a certain chaplain, gives seizin of the advowson to the Bishop of Winton, who puts in a personage by name, Roger de Molton. The Queen (who may have been Eleanor, the wife of Edward I.) proceeded against him, and gained her cause. The unfortunate bishop had to pay a fine of £20, for unlawful claim of patronage.

The queen most probably prosecuted through the king's absence in Wales or Scotland. If, however, the queen was the queen-mother, widow of Henry III., she held the town in dower for life, and claimed all the patronage connected with God's House.

CHAPTER IV.

AFTER the previous short chapter, it is now time to
shew the favour with which our " Hospital " was
treated by royal and other personages.

Now, although God's House was founded a few
years before the death of Henry II., it is curious
(as I have already observed on a former page) that
there is no mention either of Gervase or his foundation in the " Itinerary " of that king. One
would have supposed that, as Henry and his sons
repeatedly embarked from Southampton for his
foreign possessions, or landed here on their return,
the " Port-reeve " would have from time to time
received them at the Royal Pier, or in some way
come in contact with that monarch. I may observe in passing, that Southampton or Portsmouth
would be chosen as the port for " taking shipping,"
inasmuch as Winchester, and not London, was
still the place of royal residence.

We must, therefore, pass on to the reign of
Richard Cœur de Lion. In a deed of grant by
that monarch to the newly-founded " Hospital,"
confirmation is made of certain lands " to God's
House, at Southampton—Domui Dei de Suthan-
tone—and to the poor folk there abiding—et
pauperibus ibidem morantibus—for the maintenance of the said poor—ad substentationem eorun-
dem pauperum." In another grant, lands at
" Gersihc " (Gussage) were made over to the
hospital. This record is the more interesting as it
not only makes over the farm, but the *farmer* also :
" the lands together with the farmer, Turstinus, and
all his following." "Turstinus et tota sequela sua."

Sequela "—" following "—probably includes wife,
children, labourers, together with the whole of the

live and dead stock, agricultural implements, goods,
and chattels. If so, we have here an illustration,
in feudal times, of the unhappy condition of the
Saxon Gurth.

King John conveys more land at Gussage to
the " Hospital." His rescript is to the following
effect : " Johannes omnibus hominibus salutem—
John, to all men health—sciatis me dedisse, et hâc
meâ cartâ confirmasse Gervesio de Hanton—know
ye that I have given, and by this my royal letter
confirmed, to Gervase of Hanton—pro homagio et
servitio suo partem illam terræ de Gersihc*—in
return for his homage and service, that portion of
land situate at Gussage, &c."

William de Redvers, Earl of Devon (1196-1216),
makes a grant of land : " totam terram de Werrore
—all that messuage starting from Werrore," not
far from " Karesbroc," and extending to " Puke-
flunt, Northwde, Medina, and Tintesflunt—pro
salute animæ meæ, &c.—for the benefit and salvation of my own soul, and that of my ancestors and
successors."

But besides these welcome grants from kings
and wealthy nobles, the monarchs aforesaid took the
"Hospital" under their special gracious protection.
Richard I. thus orders : " Suscipimus etiam in
custodiâ et protectione nostrâ eandem Domum—
we also take under our guardianship and protection
the aforesaid house—prohibentes firmiter ne quis ei
aut hominibus suis aliquam faciat injuriam aut
molestiam aut gravamen—forbidding under severe
penalties any one to bring harm, or trouble, or in-
convenience to it or its people."

King John utters a similar severe rescript : " We
take under our care, protection, and guardianship
the Hospital of Suthamtone, its brethren, lands,
people, affairs, accounts, and all its possessions ;
and we promise to hold, guard, and protect the

* Called also Girsiche and Gersiz.

D

aforesaid house with all that appertains to it, as though it were our own royal demesne—quasi Dominicam nostram."

Henry III. accorded the same royal patronage and protection in almost the same words, which need not therefore be repeated.

In the reigns of Edward I. and II., we come across the three following items, which will relieve these somewhat dry details.

Burial of Juliana of the Island (*temp.* Edward I.), expenses incurred by Domus Dei :—

1 lb. Cotoun Candle	....	2d.
Oblations	....	1d.
Puteus (the grave)	....	1d.
Chust (coffin)	....	10d.
4 Bearers	....	2d.
Bedesmanne	.. . .	½d.

Kitchen expenses on Christmas Day at God's House (*temp.* Edward II.) :—

Noumbles, or Intestines of Deer		2d.
4 Wodekocs	... .	6d.
Larkes, Thrushes, &c.....	....	7½d.
4 Rabbits	....	8d.
120 Egges	....	12d.
14 lbs. of Paris Candles	....	21d.

The Warden gives a dinner to the Burgesses.

Pain Demesne (finest flour)	....	4d.
3 Gallons of Wine	....	16d.
Beef and Veal	....	14d.
One Tiche*	....	8d.
6 Capons	....	16d.
12 Hennes	....	2s. 0d.
240 Egges	....	12d.
Milk	....	2d.

* In an old chronicle of the 12th century, the word "Ticcen" or "Ticchen" is found, of which "hædus" is given as the equivalent Latin. Anglice "kid."

Wildefowle	....	....	....	6d.
Boy to seeke wildefowle in the				
Island	....	....	....	4d.

On the above the following brief remarks may be made. " Chust " or chest for " coffin " finds an illustration in the heading of Gen. l. " Joseph dieth and is chested." " Juliana of the Island," was one of the " Sisters." Her name is frequently to be found in the old records. There was a Juliana, an abbess of Romsey in the year 1199 ; a Juliana, wife of Roger of Shollyng (Sholing), in 1274 ; and a Juliana, wife of Ralph le Futur, who made a grant of two pounds and a half of pepper per annum to God's House.*

We now come to the eventful reign of Edward III., 1327-1377. It was eventful not only for our " Hospital," but for England also, and indeed for all Europe. In his day the " Good Parliament," which redressed many grievances, met. The commercial or great middle class took its rise. Through many and various causes real progress in learning was made, and national education, if it was not actually born in that era, at least received a power-ful impetus and grew vigorously.

What William of Wykeham afterwards did in the south, Robert de Eglesfield accomplished, in a great degree, for the north, of England.

William of Wykeham founded Winchester Col-lege, *circ.* 1387, and affiliated it to his newly-erected College at Oxford, *circ.* 1386, then and since known

---

* About the same date a pauper, unnamed, belonging to the establishment, was buried, but his funeral cost only 2½d. As we read of " Juliana of the Island," so we find a " Matillidis of the Island," a dairy-maide, who is transferred to one of the farms. Among these ancient records there is mention of a murrain break-ing out at this time among the cattle. Two of these diseased beeves were slaughtered ; of which one was immediately dressed for the table, the other was transferred to the larder ! We do things differently now-a-days.

as New College. Robert de Eglesfield had founded,
about forty years before, *circ.* 1340, the Queen's
Hall, now known as Queen's College, Oxford, so
naming it after Queen Philippa, to whom he was
then chaplain. In his College, at Oxford, he
allowed certain privileges to Grammar Schools in
the " North Countree," where he was born and
bred, and in this way provided a " liberal
education " for the sons of the farmers, " states-
men," and gentry, who lived in those wild, and at
that time almost inaccessible, counties of Cumber-
land and Westmorland. But his College, somewhat languishing through lack of funds both for
building and maintenance, he used his influence
with his royal mistress, who should try to persuade
the king to bestow the " Hospital " of God's House,
with all its valuable lands, possessions, and appurtenances, upon the lately-founded Queen's Hall,
at Oxford.* In this the good queen was successful ;
and it proved a mutual benefit to both foundations,
especially to God's House by a strange, providential,
and at the time unknown and little dreamt of, an-
ticipation. The College was permanently enriched
and flourished apace. The "Hospital" in after
years escaped confiscation under Henry VIII., on
the plea that its revenues were transferred to purposes of learning and education. No change
appears to have been made by Robert de Eglesfield
in the original object of its foundation by Gervase,
nor in its internal arrangements. Indeed, the
College was to maintain all the burdens imposed
upon the original foundation.

Of the Hospital called God's House, in the
Town of Southampton : a Charter of King Ed-

* The fact was that for many years the wardenship was merely
a wealthy sinecure. The wardens were rarely if ever resident.
They lived at Winchester, Salisbury, Odiham, Finchhampstead,
and other places than God's House. No doubt this had been
noticed by others, besides Robert de Eglesfield ; and rendered
his petition the more easy to be granted.

ward III., regulating and confirming the grants of
donors :—

"The King, &c. The grant or confirmation
which Master Roger of Hampton, the son of Gervasius of Hampton, made by his charter to God and
to the Hospital at Hampton, which is called God's
House, for a free and perpetual alms of all the lands,
revenues, and buildings in and without the town of
Hampton, which the same Gervasius granted and
conceded to the said God's House. Moreover, the
grant, gift and confirmation which the same Roger
made by another, his own charter, to the Hospital
for a free, &c. The gift, &c., which Margerie de
Redveriis made, &c., by her charter to the same
Hospital for a free, &c."

[And so on through several pages, the names
of the donors and of the lands, &c., granted
to the Hospital of God's House.]

"Edward, by the grace of God, King of England, &c.

"Be it known that when Philippa, Queen of
England, our well-beloved Consort, moved by a
charitable design, had founded anew a certain hall
at Oxford for scholars, chaplains, and others, with
our permission, and had ordained and established
certain charities to be used for the health of Ourself,
our Consort, and our children, as long as we live
upon earth, and for our souls, and for the souls of
our offspring when we shall have departed this life,
to continue always, and when the same our Consort
had provided the said Hall with certain possessions for the maintenance of the Provost and
Scholars of the said Hall, and for the support of
burdens incumbent upon the same, she had intended, God inspiring her, to give and assign
possessions more fully to the aforesaid Hall, and to
the Provost, Scholars, and their successors.

"We, commending the pious and wholesome

design of our Consort in this matter, and desiring especially to participate with the same our Consort in so righteous a work, by our special favour, and for the better carrying out of the intention of the same our Consort in this matter do grant to the aforesaid Provost and Scholars the wardenship of our Hospital St. Julian, at Southampton, called God's House, which hospital indeed exists under our patronage, to be possessed, ordered, and held by the said Provost, Scholars, and their successors, with all its privileges for ever ; with this condition, that the aforesaid Provost, Scholars, and their successors should be bound to provide for all expenses connected with the foundation from the surplus of their expenditure, if there should be any ; and also to provide a certain abode of refuge or dwelling-place for the retention of scholars of the aforesaid Hall, if any should happen to be afflicted with constant sickness or incurable disease, and also that they be bound always to increase the ordinary number of scholars now in the said hall, if the surplus should suffice for this. And it shall be the duty of the said Provost to enter the said Hospital upon the decease or resignation of the present Warden, and to hold the wardenship without let or hindrance of us or of our heirs.

> " Witness the signature of the King, at the Tower of London, in the 17th year of our reign in England, and the 5th in France."
> [A.D. 1344.]

It will be observed that henceforth the Warden of God's House is no longer an *individual*, but Queen's College, in its corporate capacity.

At the same time, Queen Philippa contributed to Queen's College a yearly rent of 20 marks for the sustenance of six Scholar-Chaplains, to be paid by her receiver.

CHAPTER V.

This splendid grant of Edward III. was confirmed and continued by subsequent monarchs. His grandson, Richard II. absolved the "Hospital" from payment of Tenths and Fifteenths. Henry IV., Henry V., and Henry VI. all favoured and smiled upon it. Henry VIth's Queen, Margaret of Anjou, and her retinue were accommodated and entertained within its hospitable walls. Edward IV. took a special interest in its welfare, chiefly for the sake of his grandfather, the Earl of Cambridge, who, as I have already observed, was buried within the Chapel. When *(App. II.)* Edward, in honour of the same Earl, his grandfather, dissociated several English religious cells from foreign monasteries, Monks Sherborne with the minor cells of Upton Gray, Bramley, and Chincham was severed from the Abbey of St. Vigor, at Cerasey, in Normandy, and affiliated to our "Hospital" of God's House. Hence, Queen's College becomes the patron of these livings. Sherborne, indeed, seems to have passed through some vicissitudes. It was first bestowed upon Eton College by its founder, Henry VI.; then transferred from Eton to God's House by Edward IV. in 1461; again, about 12 years after re-granted to Eton; and finally, it was bestowed upon and confirmed by the same king to God's House.

A charter of King Edward IV., concerning the alien Priory of Shurburne, granted to the aforesaid Hospital :—

"The King, &c. Be it known that by our special favour and for the augmentation of religious education in our Hospital of St. Julian, called God's House, in our town of Southampton, also that our well-beloved in Christ, John Perasone, now Warden of the aforesaid Hospital, as well as the Chaplains and Brothers of the same Hospital, and their successors, may the more be especially bound to pray for our health, and that of our heirs and successors, whilst we live amongst mortals, and also for our souls when we shall have gone the way of all flesh, also for the souls of that Prince of worshipful memory, the late Richard Duke of York, our father, and of the late Richard Earl of Cambridge, our grandfather, buried in the same Hospital, and of all other our progenitors for ever, we have given and granted, and by these presents do give and grant for ourselves and our heirs, as far as in us lies, to the aforesaid the present Warden, Chaplains and Brothers of the aforesaid Hospital and to their successors, the alien Priory of Shurburne, in the county of Southampton, with all and each its appurtenances, appendages, also with lands, tenements, revenues, serfs, fiefs, and advowsons in any way connected with or appertaining to Courts of Law. We give and grant the aforesaid Priory, with all other and each its appurtenances to be had and held by the aforesaid present Warden, Chaplains, &c., as a free and perpetual bounty, for ever exempt from all tax to be rendered to us or to our heirs for regal dues.

> " In token of which witness the sign manual of the King, at Westminster, the 16th day February." [No date.]

If Richard Cœur de Lion and Edward IV. only knew that " Turstinus and his " Sequela " and the " serfs " of the present day had now votes!

So matters went on until the reign of Henry VIII.; and I have already noted how it happened that the " Hospital " escaped the usual disestablishment and disendowment of religious houses.

Its varied properties were assessed at the following values by his commissioners :—

		£	s.	d.
Gussage		18	16	8
Cosseham		5	6	8
Warror		5	2	0
Ewskbury (Exbury)		0	11	8
Hekeley		3	6	10
Winton (a garden)		0	1	4
Shirborne Monastery		50	11	3
Suthantone		64	3	8
		£148	0	1

A few other items raised the sum total to £161 7s. 2d.

The following notice, couched in rather curious English, was issued by Edward VI. :—

" Three stipends founded there to be continued for ever ; three stipendiary priests, who have every one of them for their salary 53s. 4d., besides meate, drink, lodging, barber, and launder, allowed for their lyving there to celebrate and minister to the poore there, the same being payed by the Provost and Fellows of Queen's College, in Oxford, which stipends have no other lyving."

The cost of this was £20 per annum, which some of the grasping commissioners tried to get hold of ; but the King at length ordered that the College be " no longer molested, vexed, or troubled " on the subject.

It is just possible that Philip of Spain visited the " Hospital " and heard mass at the Chapel, when he landed at Southampton to proceed to Winchester for his marriage there to Queen Mary. After her brief reign Elizabeth ascended the throne, and confirmed the grant of the Hospital to the College, in whose possession it has ever since remained undisturbed.

Dr. Speed tells us that " the ' Hospital ' was in the hands of the crown in Queen Elizabeth's time.'"

If this was the case, there is nothing improbable
in the matter ; for at the beginning of every reign
it was usual for all charters to be surrendered and
granted again by the new monarch. We have
seen to what perils and dangers it was exposed
with all other religious foundations during the
reign of Henry VIII., and the Queen may have
still held the " Hospital" in her own hands until
she had consulted Burleigh and other counsellors.
Dr. Speed goes on to intimate that a certain
" Francis Mylles "—described in a family Bible
as of Bitterne and God's House—who had been
educated at Queen's College, used his influence
at Court, so " that the ' Hospital ' with all its
appurtenance was restored by a new grant to the
College."

In this statement there is nothing unlikely,
although it cannot be proved by documentary
evidence. But a letter has been found in the
Cecil Papers at Hatfield from a Francis Mylles—no
doubt the same individual—asking Walsingham,
whose secretary he had been, for the office of Clerk
of Requests. *This letter is dated from God's House.*
Probably Mr. Mylles was one of the Stewards.

An Act for the Confirmacion of Her Mties.
Lrẽs Patent graunted to the Queenes Colledge in
Oxforde.

" In most humble and lamentable wyse shewen
unto yor. most excellent Mtie. yor. faythfull and
moste obedient subiects Henrie Robynson Clerke
Bacheler of Dyvinitie Provost and the Scollers of
the Queenes Colledge in the Universitie of Oxford
that whereas the said Colledge was heretofore
erected by Robert Eglesfilde Chaplain to Queene
Philipp Wief to Kinge Edwarde the Thirde one
of yor. Highnes most noble Pgenitors and for ever
by Him dedicated and comended to the most
notable proteccion of the Queenes of this Realme.

And whereas by the varietie and multiplicitie of names of incorporaion of the sayde colledge conteyned as well in sudrie graunts unto them made as also in sundrie sutes as well bye them as against them had and pursued divers doubtes, questions, and ambiguities have heretofore risen contrarie to the meaninge of the first graunters and contrarie to equitie and good conscience, &c., &c., at the humble sute and peticon of yor. faithfull Councellors Sir William Cecil, Knt., Chancellor of Cambridge Universitie, Sir Robert Dudley, Chancellor of Oxforde Universitie, and Sir Francis Walsingham, Knt., yor. Maties principall Secretarie did for yor. Highnes Heirs and Successors incorporate the saide Colledge in deede and name to be a body pollitique and corporate by the name of the Provost and Scollers of the Queene's Colledge in the Universitie of Oxforde. And that they and their Successors should by that name have a perpetual succession. And did further by your said Ltrēs Patent give graunte and confirme unto the sayde Provoste, &c., all and singular mannors, landes, tenements, hereditaments, Advowsons of Churches, Parsonages, impropriate Knights fees, franchises, Libties, profitts, quarries, mynes, woodes, underwoodes, rentes, reversions, tythes, as well greate as smalle offerings, oblacōns, free chappells, chauntries, emoluments, profitts, &c. And whereas also yor. Highnes by yor. sayde Lrēs. Patent did graunte unto the saide Provoste and Scollers of the Queene's Colledge in the Universitie of Oxforde, who heretofore by the gifte of the saide Kinge Edwarde the Thirde were proprietories of the Hospitall of St. Julyan, commonly called God's House, in the Towne of Southamptone, that they should from the date of the saide Ltrēs Patent for ever be named and incorporated in deede and name by the name of the Provost and Scollers of the Queene's Colledge in the Universitie of Oxforde,

44

Warden of the Hospitall of God's House in the
Towne of Southamptone, and that they and their
successors by that name should have a perpetuall
successyon, and should likewise by that name
have, enjoy, and retayne to them and their successors all their landes, tenements, and hereditaments whatsoever unto the sayde Hospitall given,
graunted, and appropriated or confirmed, or intended to be unto them given, &c., by the sayde
Ltrēs Patent more at large yt dothe and may appear that now it may be ordeyned, established, and
enacted by yor. Highnes with the assent of the
Lordes, Spirituall and Temporall, and the Cōmons
in this present Parliament assembled, and by the
aucthoritye of the same that yor. Highnes saide
Ltrēs Patent and all and every graunte clawse,
artycle, and sentence therein mencioned as concerning the saide two several names of corporacōn
therein expressed, and the grante of their saide
lands, &c., may and shall from henceforth by auc-
thoritie of this present Parliament be allowed,
certified, established, and confirmed, and to be
holden for ever hereafter firme and stable according
to the tenor and trewe meaninge of the same."

Letters Patent granted at Westminster, xxij
day of October. in the xxvj year of her
reign, A.D. 1584. Confirmed by Act of Parliament in the following year.]

Four years after, viz., in 1588, the Queen grants
a warrant, signed by Her and addressed to Burleigh,
dated July 16th, in which there is permission given
to cut down fifty trees in the New Forest for the
repairs of God's House—free of charge.

"Whereas We be credibly informed that the
Hospital called God's House in our Town of
Southampton and belonging to our College in Oxford called Queen's College, by us lately established,
is by reason of the great and ancient continuance
of the same grown to great ruinousness, and our

said College also is in so poor estate that they are
not without some relief able to repair the same in
convenient sort for the habitation of the poor maintained there.—We," &c., &c.   (*Cecil Papers.*)

CHAPTER VI.

WE now come in touch with the Huguenots. For
during the reign of Queen Elizabeth these peaceful
invaders streamed over to this country in their
thousands, and, some of them settling in Southampton and the neighbourhood, the Chapel of St.
Julian, at God's House, was assigned to them as
their place of worship.

Before, however, we dwell at length on this interesting community and their connection with that
chapel, so well known at the present day as " The
French Church," it will not be out of place to draw
the reader's attention to the condition of the trade
of Southampton during her reign and the reigns of
her predecessors.

Commercial enterprise arose in very early times,
even before the later Crusades bold adventurers
from time to time braved the perils of the sea, and
risked the probable chances of meeting fierce
vikings, pirates, and other " kings of the oar," who
acted on the " good old plan " that

> " They should take who have the power,
> And they should keep who can."

The successful escape of the few amply repaid the
merchants their venture. But the Crusades especially opened men's eyes to the glories of Eastern
fabrics and luxuries, and instilled into their martial
minds the wholesome idea that there was something
better than knocking each other about and breaking
each other's heads. Venice and other cities and
towns on the Adriatic were first and foremost in

Eastern enterprise, and Venice left memorials of
herself in the west. She had a consul in Southampton. North Stoneham possesses a somewhat
mysterious ledger-stone in her church, having the
following words engraved on it :

"Sepultura della schola dei Schiavoni, A.D. 1493."

This at least points to a school, guild, or community of Dalmatian or Sclavonian sailors or
chapmen. But no information has yet been vouch-
safed to explain the origin of this grant. How
came these foreigners to have a place of sepulture
at this little village church ? As there was a great
traffic carried on by means of pack-horses and
other beasts of burden between Southampton and
Winchester in that century, and as there were frequent feuds between these foreigners and the
English, it is just possible that during one of these
fierce quarrels, sepulture was denied the intruders
at either end, and that some benevolent John of
Flanders—himself a merchant and foreign resident
at North Stoneham—may have, through sympathy
and to promote peace, granted these Dalmatians
permission to bury their dead within the consecrated
precincts of that little country church. North
Stoneham lies about five miles north of Southampton, and at that period the high or main road
between Southampton and Winchester passed
through that village and close along the church.
This, however, is merely a conjectural suggestion ;
and, therefore, with our present lack of evidence
we must leave the Sclavonians and their ledger-
stone to peaceful obscurity.

To continue our story. The municipal records
speak of " Galeys de Venece " and " Carreckes de
Jene or Jeane," probably Genoa. Ragusa, on the
Dalmatian coast, distorts her name for us and be-
queaths to future generations a remembrance of
herself in the word " Argosy." Dalmatia, too,

through the royal robe of her queens, presents the western church with the priestly vestment, the "Dalmatic."

Venetian trade with Southampton is first mentioned in the reign of Edward II., flourished till that of Henry VIII., when the export of wool was forbidden, and gradually dwindled down to a mere nothing in the days of Good Queen Bess, A.D. 1569.

In early days England was invaded by a peaceful army from another direction. The Flemings as early as the reign of Henry II., began to introduce their wares and manufactures, and to exchange them for English wool. Wool, as we are reminded by the name given to the Lord Chancellor's seat in the House of Lords, was the staple produce of our land, and was said to surpass for fineness any like production of the Continent. Sugar, with which the Crusaders had become acquainted through the Saracens in Sicily, Crete, and Syria, and to which Chaucer makes allusion : "Sugre that is so trye,"*i.e.* excellent, "And yiue (give) hem sugre, hony, breed and milk," was exchanged for this commodity. A Venetian merchant in the year 1319 shipped 100,000 lbs. of sugar, which had been brought from the Levant, and 10,000 lbs of sugar-candy, to England to receive back its equivalent in wool. Wool was bartered with Spain for Arab horses through the Flemings. Indeed, these enterprising merchants spread as far south as the Azores, where the quaint little village of Flamengoes still exists, founded by a colony of Flemings sent out by the Duchess of Burgundy in the year 1467. The Flemings, however, were much hampered by various exactions and prohibitions until the reign of Edward III., who, chiefly for political reasons against France, gave to them full protection, which enabled them to grow rich. Southampton, unfortunately, did not reap the full harvest of their enterprise, as they landed their cargoes at other ports also—as for instance, those on the east coast, as also at the Cinque Ports. This town, however, was one of the ports from which wool was allowed to be exported, and the present electric crane—such is modern progress—may be regarded as a sort of successor to the tron, under the custody of the Earl of Warwick, which was set up on the quay for the weighing of the wool before exportation.

We might be tempted to believe that the neighbouring village of Woolston, with its " Woolpack Inn," derived its name from, and was a reminiscence of, this useful and general commodity. But derivations are coy, seductive, and treacherous. In ancient records this modest suburb appears under the names of Ulmeston, Ulreston, Ulverston, Woolveston, before it finally subsides and rests in Woolston. We must, therefore, rather trace its name to the enemy of the " woolly flock " through the Swedish " ulf," the Anglo-Saxon " wulf," and the German and Dutch " wolf." I need hardly remind my readers of the Morecambe-Bay Town of Ulverston, the pretty legend of Ulswater Lake, Good Bishop Ulf-ilas, and the varied history and vicissitudes of Wolvesey Castle and Palace in Winchester.

To conclude; " in the reign of Elizabeth trade was at a very low ebb in the town, and Southampton was reckoned among the decayed ports. Its vessels were let out on hire, as there was no use for them in the port." Nevertheless, as soon as she ascended the throne, hopes and expectations ran high. The good time was coming—was already come, and poets sang :—

> " Pray we, therefore, both night and day,
> For Her Highnes, as we bee bounde:
> Oh Lorde, preserue this braunch of bay,
> And all her foes with force confounde ;
> Here long to lyue, and after death
> Receyue our Queene Elizabeth."

CHAPTER VII.

Such was the condition of the trade of the town in the reign of Queen Elizabeth. But though the commerce in wool seems to have reached at this time a state of stagnation, yet trade, both here and elsewhere, received a certain impetus from the immigration of the Huguenots to this country. Charles the IXth., King of France, and Alva, Spanish Governor and Commander-in-Chief in Flanders, were doing their best by their cruelties to bring the respective countries to ruin. So true is it that " God has ordained laws which none can set aside ; and every evil deed contains within it the seeds of punishment, and the germs of disaster and perhaps even of destruction." Huguenotism, with all its faults, contained in itself and was representative of three great principles, which took years to mature and are at last bearing fruit in our own day—viz., an Open Bible in the vulgar tongue, Freedom of Speech, and Liberty of the Press. Consequently, the Massacre of St. Bartholomew (A.D. 1572) and Alva's merciless policy were as imbecile as they were cruel. The effects were simply disastrous both at the time and two centuries later. For as the Roman moralist tells us, " Fate clings to the doer of evil and tragic deeds with unyielding tenacity, and, overtaking him at last in the person of his descendants, takes her revenge with fearful and unerring certainty."—

> "With solemn pace and firm, in awful state
> Before thee* stalks inexorable Fate ;
> And grasps empaling nails and wedges dread,
> The hook tormentous, and the melted lead."

* i.e. Fortune.

E

Fate—that is, the necessary outcome and evolution of cause, the natural transgression of God's moral laws, overtook France and her King in 1793.

Some of the results, however, were immediate and ruinous both to France and Flanders. Each country was to a great extent depleted of its inhabitants. The Huguenots swarmed into England, many by way of the Channel Islands, Guernsey, Jersey, Sark, and Origny. (This last must not be confounded with the *Orkney* Islands—as some writers mistakenly have done. It is simply Aurigney's Isle, that is Alderney). With them they brought their industry, their skill, their genius, their love of liberty, their obedience to law. With them, too, came manufactures of various kinds, the artistic creations of the scientific mind. Bankers, gold and silver smiths, glass manufacturers, paper makers, weavers, fullers,—diligent and enlightened men of all stations and ranks poured into England, set up their trades and businesses, according as they might be allowed, intermarried with the people, and virtually turned themselves into Englishmen. As regards Southampton, " the Town received a circle of persons of consideration, of which the centre lay hard by, at Rookley, Lord Galway's house." He was buried in Micheldever Churchyard, but his gravestone cannot now be found. " The colony he attracted long preserved the high-bred character which he imparted to it, was worthily maintained by Philibert D'Hervard or Herward, Baron of Huningen, once William III's Envoy to Geneva. Southampton had also received from the days of Edward VI. an unbroken influx of refugees from the Channel islands and the ports of Northern France. Their numbers were now swelled by the emigrants from Normandy, Upper Languedoc, and Poitou." Gerard de Vaux was the owner of a paper mill at South Stoneham. A petition was sent in to the Mayor and Corporation for permission to erect a mill for weaving silk and grogram-yarn in Southampton—but the result of the petition is not recorded. It was probably successful; as such a mill was erected in Winkle Street. Its site cannot now be traced; but it may have supplanted the "Infirmary," or the "Refectory" of the God's House "Hospital." Like those useful institutions it passed away, having done its work, and brought untold benefits to the community in its day and generation.

The names of La Trobe, La Touche, Labouchere, Lefevre, Le Feuvre and Faber, Breton, De Teissier, Bouverie, Moens, Layard, and last but not least, Portal, are all evidences of the immigration and settlement of the Huguenots in this country.

The derivation of the word "Huguenot" is somewhat obscure. It has been suggested that there was a leader Hugo, or Herguan, a Count of Tours. One of the four gates of Tours was called Faugon, i.e. feu Hugon, the late Hugon, and in secret vaults near this gate the Huguenots are said to have met in the night time. The name has been also traced to Aignos (which actually occurs), Aignots, Eidgenossen, *i.e.*, Confederates.

CHAPTER VIII.

In this concluding chapter we have now to speak of the connection of the Huguenots with the Chapel of St. Julian, attached to the " Hospital of God's House."

Mr. Smiles, in his "History of the Huguenots," says : " Southampton was resorted to at an early period by the fugitives from the persecutions in France and Flanders. . . . Like the two foreign Protestant Churches in London . . . . that at Southampton was established in the reign of Edward VI., when an old chapel in Winkle Street, near the Harbour, called Domus Dei, or God's House, was set apart for the accommodation of the Refugees."

Mr. R. S. Poole writes thus : " The Church of God's House, near the Harbour, had of old been their property, and it still preserves the record of former exile and of its refuge here." And again —" The Church of Southampton, composed of Walloons, of fugitives from the Channel Islands and Northern Provinces of France, was established by letters patent of Edward VI. and Elizabeth."

Upon these statements the Rev. J. Silvester Davies, in his " History of Southampton," remarks as follows : " It has been a constant tradition in the congregation that a French Church was established at Southampton by Letters Patent of King Edward VI. *But no such letters are forthcoming.*" Now King Edward died July 6, 1553. If, then, these letters existed, how is it that these Walloons are petitioning the Corporation some 14 years after, viz., in 1567, not only to have free exercise of their trades, but also to have a church assigned to

them, wherein they could worship God according to
the ' religion and administration ' as it was used in
the time of King Edward VI. ? The Corporation,
however, refer them to the Ordinary. The Ordinary
or Bishop of Winchester at that time was Robert
Horne, who has left an unenviable name by pulling
down the Chapter House and Cloisters of his own
Cathedral. The Bishop favoured the petitioners,
as also did Grindal, promoted about the same year
from York to Canterbury. Cecil's notes upon the
petition are not altogether favourable; and he gives
a strong hint that the Walloons must conform
either to the ' use ' of the Strangers' Church in
London, or to that of the English Church. At
length, however, through the interposition of Bishop
Horne with Cecil and the Council, 'they were to
have the same privileges for strangers as Sandwich
had.'   Accordingly, we find a congregation of
Walloon strangers settled in the Chapel of God's
House before the close of the year 1567, at which
period the register of the French church com-
mences, and, as we learn from several entries in
that volume, the same year was that of their ad-
mission into Hampton.   Regular services appear
to have commenced on December 21, 1567, the
sacrament on that day being received by seventy-
nine members of alien families, besides six other
members native born.   On the same day a
baptism was celebrated."

" We do not know," continues Mr. Davies, " by
what several steps they obtained footing within the
Chapel of God's House, or many questions might
have been avoided in times past.   Letters Patent
from Queen Elizabeth have been alleged, under
which it is believed that this congregation was established as one of the seven Walloon Churches,
and somehow or other was gifted to a great extent
with the Hospital Chapel. *But no such letters can
be found*, and we conclude that the congregation, as

such, was simply protected by a royal licence ; while, for the place of their meeting, they must have obtained the permission of Queen's College, to which body the entire " Hospital," and its Chapel or Chapels belongs." Dr. Speed also writes on the French congregation, in 1608 : " They still have, by leave of Queen's College and the licence of the Bishop of Winchester, the use of the Chapel of God's House, which is usually called the French Church or Chapel." In the year 1712 the College threatened to forbid them the use of the Chapel, unless they conformed to the Anglican " use "—for of course the Walloons were, according to the law of England, Dissenters—and it was added that the College felt that the Chapel had been put to a bad use in serving for their assemblies. The College, too, has always done the structural repairs. From these two facts alone, even in the absence of all written evidence, the natural inference is that the College enjoys *possession* of the Chapel together with the rest of God's House. Whereas the French congregation enjoys *occupation* only, and even that is subject to the will and consent of the College.

Synods were established in 1581, by the Huguenot Church, in London, and attended by members of the Church in Southampton.

The *Registers* contain many interesting items. They commence in 1567 with the list of communicants, who in the first year number fifty-eight. In 1665 this number has dwindled down to three— the plague seems to be responsible for this—and here the list closes. " Temoinage," or some such word, written against names, means that they brought written or other testimony to their being Protestants. " Messe," that they had attended mass under compulsion.

The *Births*, or rather *Baptisms* (1567), begin with two entries, and in 1677 reach to thirty, and cease altogether in 1799. In the thirty-three years previous to this last date, the whole number had been only twenty-one.

The *Marriages* commence in 1569 and cease in 1753. The curious thing is that very few of the names among the baptisms occur again in the list of marriages.

The *Deaths* begin in 1567. The first entries are very short, merely giving the names. From time to time the word " peste " is added. The register ends in 1722. Many of the ministers were buried in the Chapel : *e.g.*, Philippe de la Motte and Paul Mercier, Adam de Cordonelle, aged 90, and his wife. Also Madame Cougot, wife of M. Cougot, first a minister at St. Julian's, afterwards rector of Millbrook, where he lies interred ; at the same time also, in 1721, the Baron of Huningen died and was buried in Holy Rood Church ; so also, I think, was the Rev. Isaac J. Barnouin in 1797.

There is a long list of *Fasts*, some seventy in all, up to 1667. The occasions of them were : the wars of William III., the war in the Netherlands, the Plague, an earthquake in England and France, and the great comet of 1581.

There were also special *Prayers* for the success of Queen Elizabeth in Ireland, for the King (William) " et sa gloire," for the Bishop of the Diocese, and for the Oppressed Protestant Churches abroad.

There are also a few *Thanksgivings*, chiefly for victories in the Netherlands.

The Huguenot or Walloon Church, as might be expected from the cessation of persecution, seems to have been gradually merged into what is now termed the French Church or Congregation. As the supply of Huguenots failed, the Chapel was still open to Protestant French-speaking people, whether of France or of the Channel Islands. Probably the conforming to the order and ritual of the Church of England in the year 1712 had something to do with this change. The regulative arrangements and the governing body appear to have been retained. And this continued until the year 1856, when the Charity Commissioners, on petition, granted a new scheme, which has been adopted and is now in use. Queen's College has nothing to do with the management of the French Congregation, nor contributes to their funds. The College merely "assigns" the Chapel to their use. They have trustees of their own, and a small endowment.

L'ADIEU.

We have now reached the end of our story, and can only regret that there are still some matters in connection with the " Hospital " which for the present must remain in doubt and obscurity for want of documentary evidence. Still, there is enough to interest us much. We have traced the history of the foundation from its very beginning, accompanied it through all its vicissitudes, and are witnesses to-day of its enlarged and permanent usefulness in the cause of education and refined culture. Some of my readers may lament, as they look back along the centuries at the original purposes of its pious founder, that the " Hospital " can scarcely lay claim to its own name, as a centre of hospital-ity to pilgrim and wayfarer; nor even in a more re-stricted sense as a temporary or permanent refuge for the sick and afflicted. Some, too, especially if archæologically inclined, will sigh the sigh which the Roman poet breathed over the site of ancient Troy, when we search in vain for the infirmary, and refectory, and the kitchen, and the pigeon-house abutting on the earthern mound over against the Friary, in Gloucester Square—

"Etiam periere ruinæ."
"Their very ruins have perished."

The present size, too, and extent, though so compact, and cosy, and picturesque, yet so shrunken in its old age, may again remind us of words written in sadness by the same Roman,

"Magni stat nominis umbra."
"It stands a mere shadow of its former noble self."

But it is just at this point that one of the guiding ideas of the late Prince Consort's life comes to the rescue, viz.: "The Beauty of Usefulness." "The principle of good," said the lamented Prince, at the opening of some schools, "once sown, is not destined to lie dormant, but like the grain of mustard seed, it is calculated to extend and develop itself in an ever-increasing sphere of usefulness; and we may confidently hope that what you have now effected, following this universal law, will not be limited in its results to the immediate objects of your charitable exertions, but that it will prove the means of diffusing untold blessings among the most remote generations."

No words can be found more applicable to describe the case of our "Hospital;" for every new step taken in the history of God's House has been a fulfilment of such sentiments expressed, inasmuch as every successive step has been one of progress— from the welcoming of pilgrims to the support and endowment of learning. Every one can see, and will rejoice to see, in its present relations to the University of Oxford, and consequently in its enlarged sphere of work and scope for action, immensely increased capacities for usefulness— usefulness indirectly to the citizens of this town, and usefulness most certainly of a very direct kind to the whole nation. "It may be that the new can be reverentially blended with the old, and the two work together side by side for the common weal. But if either should be called to give place, it will certainly be the old; the new must reign in harmony

with the requirements and demands of the civilized
life of modern days. Yet even in such a case, the
old will live again in the new, and it is this renew-
ing of itself which brings to English institutions
greatness, stability, and permanence. Thus the
great traditions of the past can be happily, wisely,
and usefully combined with the highest aspirations
of the present and future."

"The old order changeth, yielding place to new,
And God fulfils Himself in many ways,
Lest one good custom should corrupt the world.'

APPENDIX.

(Unknown) FATHER = MOTHER (Unknown)

ROGER   GERVASE = ISABELLA
(1st Warden).

(?) BERENGARIUS = ?   ROGER = ?

WALTER   THOMAS   AZON = ? Perhaps the first
(Heres Gervasii).   Mayor of Southampton, 1205,
    and re-elected in 1217

WILLIAM DE BAGGEWORDE   RALPH   JOHN
BENEDICT (3rd Mayor), 1237-48.

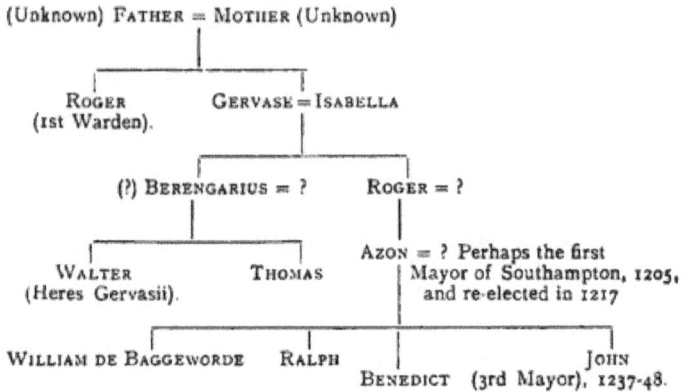

On account of the scantiness of the records,
the above " Stemma " is only approximately
correct.

1. We are quite ignorant, as yet, of the names
of the sons' and grandsons' wives.

2. The son of Gervase was also called
" Master Roger, of Southampton."

3. Walter and Thomas are said to be
" nepotes " of Gervase. This word may be translated either " grandchildren " or " nephews ; " but
as Walter is called " the son of Berengarius, and
heir of the aforesaid Gervase," and signs the deed
of sale with Isabella, it is not unreasonable to
suppose that he was the eldest son of Gervase's
eldest son, and that Berengarius had died in early
life, or was killed in battle. About this time there
was a Berengarius defeated and killed by the Huns
in North Italy.

4. Roger had certainly a son, Azon. Now,
in the year 1205 Southampton was incorporated—

shortly after the death of Gervase. Curiously, the name of the first and second chief magistrates is only a matter of conjecture. But there looms mistily through the haze and fog of centuries a tradition that the first mayor was a certain Nicolas Azon, a valiant Crusader. Azon, I suspect, is a descriptive surname, to be found under other forms, such as Agon and Acon, all three being akin to Accho, or Acre. Acon (I find in an old Gazetteer) was "the name of a guild or body of Crusaders, who attached themselves to the Knights Hospitallers." Is it altogether improbable that they founded and built the Church of St. Nicolas Acons, in the City of London?* (St. Nicolas was a Norse Saint.) The inference is that the burgesses of this town chose as their first chief magistrate Nicolas (L') Azon, *i.e.*, Nicolas, the Crusader of Acre, and that he was the grandson of the Founder of God's House.

Of Berengarius I can find no mention. But if we remember that Richard Coeur de Lion's Queen was Berengaria, Princess of Navarre, and that there was a notable Azon, Margrave of Este (an ancestor of our Queen), living at the end of the tenth century, it is quite possible that Gervase was royally connected.

I.

THERE is the following interesting notice of Gervase, which I have omitted to incorporate into

* The Church of St. Nicolas (or Nicholas) Acons, in the City of London, was founded about the year 1084. The Acon Company of the Crusaders was a branch of the Templars: its full title was, "Militia Hospitalis S. Thomœ Martyris Cantuariensis de Acon." A "Hospital" was founded by Becket's sister, in Cheapside, for a Master and Brethren of this order in the reign of Henry II. We may reasonably infer, therefore, that the Church stood in the same relation to this Acon Guild that the "Temple Church" did to the Templars: and its contiguity to the "Hospital" rendered it easy for this "agnomen," surname, or descriptive title to be attached to the Saint's name. It was thus also possible to distinguish it from its sister-church, St. Nicolas *Olave*.

the body of this work, and relegated to an appendix, as there is some need of explanation.

"Gervase, Provost of Sudhanton, returns the assessment of the old farm, at Sudhanton, at cccclvi. li. iijs. ixd. bl., and of the new farm, at Sudhanton, at ccli. li." *temp.* Rich. I.

(*a*) This old and new farm are unknown.

(*b*) li. = libræ, or pounds (in weight).

(*c*) bl. is an abbreviated form of blanco or blancum, *i.e.*, money blanched or whitened by some alloy—possibly silver—so that it was of a lighter colour than bronze and other money. Curiously, this amalgam seems to have depreciated its value; for a bill incurred by the King's sons, to the tune of £68 3s. 8d., cannot be cleared for less than £71 11s. 8d. if paid in this blanched coin. About 5 per cent. was added for weight lost in the process of dealbation.

2. The King's Yacht in mediæval Latin is "Regis esnécca." These boats were long, narrow, and fast sailers, a sort of galley with a snake-like motion, built for quick voyages to the King's foreign dominions. The word esnecca seems to be derived from A.S. snaca or snacu; Sanscrit, snag; Danish, snekke; Icel. snekkja, *i.e.* a snake; whence the old English "snack," now called "smack," a fishing-boat. In process of time, letters get altered and interchanged—thus, the monks always wrote Letley, *i.e.* Netley, Abbey; "Lunch" is, again, really Nunch or Noonch, *i.e.* the noon-tide meal.

3. Vikings, p. 45.—These were the Norse and Danish Sea Kings of olden time. The word is generally mispronounced vi-king, as though "vi" were a sort of equivalent for "sea." It should be pronounced "vik-ing," *i.e.* people who live in "viks," or "wicks." These were fortified villages built on the banks of fiords or rivers some miles inland, where these rovers could keep their plunder in safety. So in England, Norwich, Dunwich, Ispwich.

As there were frequently salt-pans near these Norse villages,—hence we find this termination to names of towns in this country connected with salt, *e.g.* Northwich, Nantwich, Droitwich.

4. Winkle Street.—God's House is now in Winkle Street. But when it was founded it stood open to the water. In the reign of Henry III., the southern town wall was built running in front of the "Hospital," from the water gate to the eastern wall, where the two walls meet at an angle. In this angle or corner is God's House Gateway, leading to the eastern suburbs. There can be little doubt, then, that the street gained its name, not from Mr. Pickwick's protégé, nor yet from that shell-fish, beloved of nursemaids and usually associated with a pin, but from O.G. Vinkel, an angle or corner.

5. Bretheren and Sisteren.—Observe the Old English plural in *en*. A few such still survive amongst us. Brethren, though not sisteren ; men, women, children, oxen ; chicken is really the plural of chick ; twin is a plural.

6. The mode of calculating the value of money is as follows :—

In the times of the Norman Kings the Silver Penny was as twenty-two and a half to eight grains, the estimated value of ours, or nearly three times as much.

In Plantagenet days, besides taking *weight* into account, we shall have to multiply the sum by at least 12 to get at its present equivalent. No doubt, many animals and wood were much cheaper than they are now.

7. The spelling of the name Southampton passes through divers vicissitudes. Suhamptone, Sudhamptone and Suthamptone (*temp.* Richard I. to Edward III.) ; Sothampton (Richard II) ; Southamptone and Suthampton (Elizabeth). In old Latin records it is known as "Hamonis Portus." The church of Holy Rood passes through similar changes

of spelling. Holly Roddes (Richard I.) ; Holy Rodes
(Edward I.) ; Holy Roods (Elizabeth) ; in last and
present century, Holy Rhood.   On one of the cha-
lices there is this inscription : " The gift of Ann
Maiier, wife of John Maiier, alderman of Holirudes,
1627."

II.

Note on " Alien Priories," by the Very Rev. the
Dean of Winchester : "The alien priories were long
a-dying.   Hook defines them as 'cells or small religious houses in our country, dependent on large
foreign monasteries.' "

So long as the interests of England and France
were not opposed, and the English King was also
lord of a good slice of France, these examples of
the taxation of England for the benefit of foreigners
went on merrily enough.   But after a time the
English kings saw no fun in letting English wealth
be paid over to England's enemies, and preferred
to take the dues themselves—subtracting the
money from France and adding it to England. The
seizure began with Edward I., in 1285, and went on
from time to time, usually when there was a war
with France on hand, till at last, in the year 1414,
the House of Commons, in a Parliament held at
Leicester, made petition to King Henry V. that
the estates of alien priories should be taken into
the king's hand (2 Henry V.), and these priories
were accordingly in large part then dissolved, and
their estates vested in the crown."

The churches of the Channel Islands were separated from the Diocese of Coutances, and attached to Winchester in 1568 (*temp*. Elizabeth).

III.

Note on the French Church or Congregation
at Canterbury, which meets for worship in the

Cathedral Crypt— by the Hon. and Rev. Canon
Fremantle.

* * * * *

" I am greatly interested in the French Church
at Canterbury, and belong to the Consistory.
There is a movement among some of our Canons
to suppress it, but I defend it. There is no
charter, and I doubt if there ever was one. But it
is known that the Walloons (French, from the Low
Countries) met there in Edward VI's reign, and it
is believed that they had royal sanction for it, as
afterwards in Elizabeth's reign. They used to
have the whole of the crypt, and to use it for
weaving, printing, schools, and worship. I believe
the only actual document they have is a decision
of the Privy Council in Charles II.'s time, signed
by the King. This was the decision of a dispute
between two sections of their own body. This
dispute was then and there settled, and the Council
added that the French Congregation should be
allowed to continue their meetings ' in the ac-
customed place *near* the Cathedral '—which no
doubt means the Crypt. The Congregation therefore claim that they have royal permission to use
that portion set apart for them, and no one can
take it away. Some years ago the Charity Commissioners tried to divert the small endowment to
beds in the hospital ; but Archbishop Tait prevailed
on the House of Lords to disallow this scheme. I
do not think they can claim a freehold, but the
right to use their part of the crypt. We are trying
to furnish services for French governesses at Folke-
stone and Dover, so as to make the Church more
useful."

www.ingramcontent.com/pod-product-compliance
Lightning Source LLC
Chambersburg PA
CBHW020242090426
42735CB00010B/1802